Horses on Drums

Horses on Drums

poems

Lawrence Bridges

 RED HEN PRESS | *Los Angeles, California*

HORSES ON DRUMS

Cover photograph: "Brewing Storm" © 2000 Barbara Van Cleave

Book and cover design by Mark E. Cull

ISBN: 1-59709-061-1
Library of Congress Catalog Card Number: 2005934167

Published by Red Hen Press

The City of Los Angeles Cultural Affairs Department, California Arts Council, Los
Angeles County Arts Commission and National Endowment for the Arts partially
support Red Hen Press.

First edition

to my wife

Contents

Sweeping the Brane

Three Years of a Good Habit

You Are Always Entertaining and Delightful

When the Industrial Revolution Ended

Introduction

Thirty years ago Lawrence Bridges was a legendary figure among poets at Stanford. Upon graduation in 1971, he had not done something sensible like get a job or go to graduate school. Instead, he had gone to New York to be a writer. Soon his work began appearing in *Poetry* and *The New Yorker*. Meanwhile bits of news surfaced second or third hand. A screenplay sold to Hollywood. An affair with a beautiful professor. Dinner parties with James Merrill, Howard Moss, Edward Albee, John Ashbery, and Penelope Mortimer. Working with Francis Ford Coppola as an assistant director on *The Conversation*. Ah, bohemia! Most of us had never met Larry, but his example was the stuff that literary dreams are made on.

My first contact with Larry came through the mail in 1973. A packet of poems arrived one day at the offices of *Sequoia*, the Stanford literary magazine, which I edited. I was only vaguely familiar with his name. His literary career had just started. I read his work, therefore, with a disinterested eye. *Sequoia* always received far more poems than it could publish, and I had no special expectations that these submissions would avoid the rejection pile. My disinterest did not last long.

It is difficult to explain to people who have not read through thousands of manuscripts submitted for publication, but editors often know whether they will publish a poem from its first line. It is not merely that few poems can survive a dull or awkward opening. Rather it is that a fully achieved poem unmistakably announces itself with the opening line, which has the music, energy, and authority that will pervade all the subsequent verses.

These poems had exactly that impact. I knew at once that afternoon that I would publish Larry Bridges' poetry. I was not surprised a few months later to see his work in *Poetry* and *The New Yorker*. Over the next few years we published him regularly in *Sequoia*. In the meantime he moved from New York to Hollywood where he worked as a film editor while his screenplay was developed into a movie.

I did not know it yet, but Larry was at the beginning of a distinguished and influential career in film and video—directing, producing, and editing.

He brought a poet's eye and ear—not to mention a sense of rhythm—to his cinemagraphic work, which was especially evident in his pioneering involvement in music videos, a form which he helped develop through his innovative editing style. When *Connoisseur* praised his work in rock videos by calling him "the Ezra Pound of post-production," the comparison was entirely apt.

During these years I often regretted that Larry had not collected his bold and dynamic early work, which combined the serpentine syntax of John Ashbery with a hard-edged intellectual fervor entirely his own. None of these fine poems survive in the present book, not even the ones published in *The New Yorker.*

If *Horses on Drums* is a first book, it is one that emerges from the mature development of a practiced poet. These newer poems mostly abandon the complex syntax of the early work to strive for a deeper complexity of meaning and method. They work by bold statement and abrupt transition, by nervously cutting from image to image. The skilled and ruthless eye of an editor is everywhere apparent.

The narrative line has been almost entirely eradicated. What remains is a dazzling procession of images, attitudes, and ideas, which exhibit a certain logic but achieve most of their meaning by implication rather than explication. These poems pose philosophical questions, but the end-effect of their argumentation is not so much clarity as mystery. The poems are enormously compressed, often tense with unresolved or even unresolvable emotion.

Horses on Drums is a dense, ambitious, and original book. Having begun in the New York School thirty-odd years ago, Lawrence Bridges now constitutes a one-man Los Angeles school. It may take the reader a few pages to get into synch with the volume's cacophony of wonders, but it is well worth the wait.

—Dana Gioia

Horses on Drums

The Sea Is a Self-Extracting Archive

Favorite Color: Green

It's all in one ear and eat my dust.
Tranquility has a plot. I'm wide-awake
Before dawn and a ship passes on lavender water.
The banked turns and sprints end in the tropics.
Vents of compressed air blast through the sand.
Nothing appears as clearly as it does in foreshadow.
It's like living an entire vacation by anticipating it.
People like statements better than questions.
It takes effort to boost the anvil of the week
To the manhole street.
I have no idea of the mind I'm in.
An empty mind has nothing to waste.
It moves as quickly through metropolis as
It does through melancholy.
It's a dangerous youth I feel.
Tall buildings pose as waterfalls.
Light poles grow fronds.

The House Is a Vegetable

Two days after the storm and the Earth's soil
Heaves into itself with cold. I could not sleep.
The tree above us became my mind.
This floating, high-speed air slamming into leaf
Is tree-speech. Fallen branch and acorn, a warning
Of widow-maker limbs and insurance claims.
The house grows pale in this weather, sick
Buckets under every leak, foolish pool appended,
And every corner a capillary race. Water drips
From ceiling fixtures day and night to show its
Luminous bearings. An aging eucalyptus, ready to fall
In a gray joust with the storm, follows me in a barrel.
The house knows its inhabitants as muddy footprints,
Shifting from side to side, squishing carpet pads,
Rippling the standing water. The children sleep
In raincoats, while the adults eat the swimming rabbits.

Reminds Me of Crossing the Cascades

Today we're on the brink of being
On the right planet, where time has one logo. Now,
Possessed by a picnic blanket of miniature terrain:
Monitor mountain, *stylo* forest, check desert.
I drift on lint to see the city of my desk, volcano
Tea and dirty book tops and the general slum
Of whim. While taking breath, I've floated adventure,
I've hollowed out a tunnel through the hill.
Signals leaking through the rock cluster
Of brain anoint the mood like a rolling stream
And liberate a civilization of clicks, sibilants, and memes.
Rain makes the joys of my yard invisible. Here $9/10$ths
Of all injuries come from bus-sized bugs. Caution,
A pincer bug was fished out, dead, from a keyboard
Crevasse. Been dead for days. But I go as high as the eye
Because, beyond, I am a man, am out of shape.
You need a circus to be this nimble.
My face has flowers.

Horses on Drums

I am slow to settle and begin the journey.
Step outside to the prairie. I've put thoughts on
The side in little corrals, looked over a fence at what's
Going on under the power lines. It's orange poppies
And a stubborn horse who won't go into the trailer
(molasses-laced oats worked). I can identify.
I like molasses, too. No one asked me how I'd
Handle it. Never bored. So what easterly is worth catching
And running? This place is gorgeous with ordinary things
At rest and this is the summer I step into from my winter retreat.
Another bumblebee flew into my room this morning
Looking for a place to sleep, and fell silent.
Dawn pulls out through the door.
Horses on drums stop the population like church bells.
Ride out now on horses, before there are roads.

Men Who Shout in Spanish

The weight of twenty-thousand days is up and alert
Like *that*. Listen. The palms are banging rain rhythms
And the sky has clouds, big deal. There isn't a name
For this time of year, except stopped. Not turning, not roasting,
Not giving up because the visitation of art and skill
Waits for another Cabrillo to sail into LA, and, therefore,
Dives between generations. Transportation and communication
Connect the planet: a wooden boat comes one way, migration
Down the beaches goes another until they meet here,
At the foot of Sunset Blvd. where I awaken to a world
Where I know everybody. The lesson book is open,
The page pattern permanent, left behind
For future lessons. Then I transport my mind in
Code, walking without feet to unknown persons,
To a time of rain and raging sea just down our street,
When so-what-clouds blew away and a ship was sitting
In the water just off shore, with men shouting in Spanish.

At the End of Sunset

The secondary noises: latch, door, dog.
The scene is still quiet
From inside. The smell of cooking
Fish that drifted down from up the street
Last night. We had fish, too. It didn't make me
Hungry, made me think how fish still race us
Through evolution. The scene is of the sea,
20,000 years, each generation in turn
Embarrassed by frustrated science, our messed-
Up town, ruined by cars. You drop your windows
And smell salt between the noise. One dog, any
Dog beats any appliance in social adaptation.
Our teeth are straight and we live longer,
But we still look at the stars and wish to break
The deadly code of DNA and live forever.
Don't you know time will meet the same dog
Over and over?

Round Trip

Here in these settled parts, the families
Suspend their genes on clotheslines, above ravines
Which agriculture, thick as pineapple fields, surrounds.
Not a moment of repose in all the years of postponement,
In sickness and health. A place to work, the beach
Cove and road through oaks was different for them,
Where the water is wide enough to be convex, showing
The degree of Earth's roundness: there was beauty
To paint, as was last night's moonrise over the bay facing
East from the far western point. Art is quaint
And meaningless in the world of change, but who
Thought poverty would be the fruit of the world?
We have made nothing of ourselves today.
The clean sea and grassy hills answer in kind: You,
In a small way, belong.

Blood Red Sunrise

Living-in-the-past-humor breaks out
And I feel excluded by getting the jokes.
It's insecurity of car, must be, due to
The reverse-reveal of arriving in cars,
Which should come at the end.
Why does this village have so many nervously
Smoking blonde women in black?
We leave and the mystery man drives off in a hybrid.
Gravity increases.
Now, the damn dog is doing the snoring.
Never accommodate a snoring dog.
It would bring danger.
The dream with the dwarf meant the middle of life is here.
If enemies are shopping, you are betrayed.
If cow eats cow, a bad year follows a good.
If you awake angry, you've chosen the wrong past.

Threaten to Be Arbitrary

This Is Not a Summer Poem

I
The sun's bottomed out for the year.

My chair is pushed to the edge
and the yard is quiet, like forgetting.
This is my morning to lean my body.
I tried the skin of ordinary living,
but no, I became a sandy beach, a mosquito's
audible exhaust, a dry breeze, mere hoeing.

I cannot taste the air.
I see the problem with dust. You see yourself
come forward in the parking lot, older
each time. The visible world is nearer at hand,
but, alas, I repeat myself; the syntax
is circular. A change of wind pushes
across our pool. All weather is wind.
I can hear the air in the trees.
I don't want to live so long I miss hearing
my requiem. Now a wind-storm

fells branches, rotates and I can smell
the city's better half. A California
where Aztec or Spaniard never reached, those days
when you know it's going to be hot. I listen
for bad habits and elevator talk as if they assumed
I was not there. I know I'll get my march
into the mouth of perplexity. I'll see that middle life
is a mountain arguing against all height for knowing stars.
But, I cannot hear my own treading.

It Starts With the Right Words

II
Sunset

traffic leaks into my room like static.
It's about arcs—me with the instant
syntax, and the one word from a century of image.
I can hear planes at the airport reverse-thrusting.
It's all for some other consciousness where
we lived in the lost years as the millennium turned, last
and first generation of Pax Mundi.
We're free. We breathe
our fill of space. It's summer in the stars.

But I cannot find my own thinking.

I have not found the lake where I'm deaf
enough, as if clocks were half-moons, the papers
turned face-down, damn brain, damn
old language that is not our tongue.
I'm a mike—all the antics and platitudes go into me.
Testing. I can act with such a tongue-in-cheek
mess around here and, getting worse, it *is* the best of times. This
might be a dying day for someone else. The phony
dialect and false ennui blown like paper with birds:

Flight by night, fight by day, awful
sleep, broken attention. This is our link
to the reptile stars, flying before we could think,
fighting before we could choose. Within the shell

of light, where nerves appear to see,
we cross from big beach ball planets
to the raw world, like an underworld,
where we don't belong and shouldn't go.
The burning man looks to you for fire.
It's there in a box and is you. I seldom enter
with a theme. But

pulling away on the commute, I recede
and shrink to the life in a pencil.

A mock ending to the start, in our ends
are our beginnings. I turn the page
for the subject and solution to my turmoil.
It's time for the slow unyielding world.

I approach my ordeal with aplomb,
forgetting in its gravity
we have death in common
with the stars.

Atomic Body

III
Everything is urgent.
But to what urgency do I owe this inspiration?
The door is closed yet lets in scent.
The world is flat and has an edge
in space. We all walk out on it
as a shelf revealed by tide.
This wandering makes us float, though
we seem to be walking the sky on free feet.

Window Jamb on the World

IV
You must agree.
You're stuck in your head of opinion. That's the wire
of the hive. I thought it was language, some adult middle
ground between hope and despair. There, the lottery
made me, thanks to luck and the Blues. I've let
the public see my wallet photos and now they are part of
the public vocabulary, part of the mother timeline, happenstance.
And in pitch dark, on TV, traffic jams downtown like morning stars.

I hope prophecy is hogwash,
because I've structured so many bad omens
without knowing it. Now, I need not from knowing,
hear more in silence, convert breath to cash,
use the word "red" too much, play
with existentialism as entertainment.
My seasons are the news, probably driven
by polls of what we want to hear. My daughter
drops the clicker into the Coke. There are more broken
things in the world than there are broken hearts.
This gloom betrays mortality. I'll find something
needing repair, pull a light over it,
make it mine.

Threaten to Be Arbitrary

V
That living hell exists with or without your content.
Why not, if wounded, enjoy the variety of hells.
        A townsman.
You should be enjoying yourself, free as you are from
performance anxiety with all your days carefree
to beam and behold and embrace.
But the hole still opens, usually at three or four or five,
and it's something you can't do anything about.
Same effect each time. Everything's wrong and you
should escape, a thrush of emotion streaming like soft air
from a heater. Now you're philosophical. Everything's right
because it's quiet.

        As I pedal uphill in the dark I see
the moon between the trees, full. I'm beginning
to see by the light of the sunrise, but it's still dangerous.
I have no lights of my own. Moon in orange moonset.
You'd wrong this for its lack of flight, but not for
its still air. Any word you say is the most important
word in your world: bi-valve. It works.

        Notes
to yourself and crossed out for a time.
I love resonance more than measure.
Such is my skin against the vacuum. I'm more
amazed I'm an atom. Yodel a doodle.

Purpose

VI

God is sex and the world is for fun. Check yes or no.
I love you, I do not qualify.
To live is to be granted one wish.
I wished for you. The changes in my body,
not mine, the place and time, not mine, but ours.
Undiscovered by myself, seeing you coming, I am you
from the inside, blind cave voice of half-night
without objects, dreamer sated with dream,
hoping the phone doesn't ring. The doctors say
the mind is an overly elaborate system
for courtship display. Peacock feathers.
I hear the words spoken as a prayer
sometime in the future. We expect
happiness or punishment. Blame
the world for having it both ways.

Now This Forest

The Butterfly Circus

The loon lake of long thought that eats weeks
Piles vehicles at its edge, surrounds the high
Mound of your refuge: it's not politics
And intellectual clarity, it's the crude hand-cranked
Flapping wheel in the back yard that wakes the town
Of thought. I go back to the time when pilgrims marched
Through Santa Fe. I did not know it, but a woman
Was laughing and twisted her face away, exposing her
Ample dentistry. A young man leaves
An older woman, which unbalances the world
For centuries. A day was starting under a day that was
Ending. I work backward. I have one thing to do
Today, to decide if it's doable at all. I'll take
The buzz of pure silence, new light
Through the peaches ripening in the south yard.
Photo of sky, photo of tree, photo of distraction.
Your goal is to dance at the intersection,
To shred your shirt, hawk the butterfly circus.

D and O Are the First Two Letters of Doubt

You turn from them as they call you to the fields.
There's no just meditation when you close your eyes.
The self-story is buffeted, too, by dream. You whittle
Other wood, of joy. You're in a tank where art is emotion
And it can't be recorded, only reported. The faint
Electric hum almost kills you, as you look for its source,
Holding your ears. What you want is to be tied to the past
And who you were. Tumble down and whittle water,
Your art is form no more. The water clouds and
The body floats as if standing, now ears above liquid.
You walk out of the surf in your neighborhood
And swim home. This is being awake:
No art, doing nothing.

What I Say When You Ask Me What I Do

Now comes the lonely plunge and last minute notes to the future,
An hour from now, in case coffee causes forgetfulness. This
Reflexive holiday-slash-examination is the darling myth of the gods
Of the garage and finds itself disesteemed by near
Traffic noise. I've ponied up for so many sure schemes.
I know the deception here. By all effects, this is legit like
The phrase "reindeer games," but that's the working stiff's
Promise for self-improvement on a given day. And television,
What else does one do, knowing that 90% of human conversation
Is gossip? I spend my idle hours in exercise, describing:
In audible and tripping pattern, the already abstract.
I like knobby tires and canoe gardens. I seem to forget
What "it" is most of the time. When I remember,
Following the same rules, I cannot mention it.

Why I Can't See It Coming

Fortune is my weather
As I rise and greet other
Living things, the bounding crows, our
Dog "roomtone."
Enough to expel the cottonballs
Of sleep and wave survivor-like, or
As high priest and free,
My own sweet machine a band and
Riverboat, my blood
The river. There is still
The memory of hearing
Frenzied coyotes killing young
Rabbits near our land
Without funeral, a screaming
Place. Behind the mountain
Is the giant of world domination
With thermonuclear device in hand.
The Rome-moves are in flux again.
I am in the stream, now
Survivor on a mid-river islet, now
A menu item floating in a wake.

The First Move

The plain reams of blue and white tailored into a summer suit
That moved with the slow walking and light wind
Honored a good friend, returning home after a six year
Journey with no goal. The figure might have been Apollo
At a picnic in a common field, or a star-sighting in a supermarket
While running down the hill to get more soda for a pool party.
All at once, the lightning-soft body in outline appeared
As if planned at the end of the short era and caused
The brain gates to hinge. The figure disappeared and left
Something behind, like the weaving of air, manner, and fabric,
And the molds for perfection and sufficiency,
Like the taste for everything when the journey is over. The still
Atmosphere waits for an eye to blink and your body to make
The first move.

Fifty Ivory Elephants

Blue corner in a white field. A million
Clones in similar stripes and you must find
The one who dropped his hat. The highlighter
Makes beams rise from the core of the Earth
Through newsprint; you cross a yellow log
And sandpaper board to cisterns for storage, data,
Friends' names. In your world you have hours,
You crash into crystal, a public paper weight,
And supply chaos with a map. This machine
Sends all your mail to everyone in the world
At once. You respond with more. A pomegranate
Seed with fifty ivory elephants inside waits
On top of a box of words you don't know.
And this is just the desktop.

Sweeping the Brane

"The new idea would not replace the Big Bang, which has for more than 50 years dominated cosmologists' thinking over how the universe began and evolved. But instead of a universe springing forth in a violent instant from an infinitely small point of infinite density, the new view argues that our universe was created when two parallel 'membranes' collided cataclysmically after evolving slowly in five-dimensional space over an exceedingly long period of time. These membranes, or 'branes' as theorists call them, would have floated like sheets of paper through a fifth dimension that even scientists admit they find hard to picture intuitively."

—Robert Roy Britt★

I
And jargon is the consequence . . .

I lean the weight
Of my entire body into words, the underspirit
In the dark, seek out conflict.
I fall forward on the snowy parapet,
A spiral wind like a long scarf, trying
To save a friend, fallen over the edge.
(Pushed back, each day becomes speech off the balcony.)
I call for help, which goes unheard.
I search for a conceit you haven't seen, mere syllables
That the static days say I lived. Till now
All my adjectives are of its nouns. This is not the ink
Of convenience, and this turn is a moment not
Unacted upon in the corner of an obscure century.
I can't say that poetry is a foreign thing,
Though I live in it like a circus kid.

II
I'm picturing myself before writing, standing
Before you, saying all quiet now, here is our core.

My speech repeats the grace of how we are loved back
By our fragile senses, all at once, again.

The darling of the world is the body,
Not the mind.

III
Now
The day breaks open and
A glass sea of involuntary speech
Comes alive inside.
The era of getting up has ended.
You're like the movie about poetry where
Everyone who appears is a poet, all
The anthology names there
And, unbelievably, thousands you never knew, who write
Poetry: the wake-up call voice-over person,
The department store clerk, the pilot,
Even a movie star.

Now
I daydream constantly. Everything
Creaks and echoes like a mountain
Of automobile hoods,
Why I awaken in panic in a flimsy junkyard.

I squeeze the thought out of flesh
As a big bug drops
On the desk and limps away: Strange science. Strange planet.
I believe we are subject to molecular rules beneath
Our minds. This guarantees our moment
Is now, and our creations, clean.

IV
The empty page has bones.

Poets play time from both ends.

How steep hope is.

V

Balloons hold me down.
Looks like a balloon rising to the catwalk
After confetti. You see,
I'm in the cups of my own clutter.
The stomach cannot think.
There, you plot the paperwork of the hour
And plan a day of endurance, not anticipation.
The phone rings like a bolt loose in a drum.
I say it gets worse
And worse, a run of O's is headed toward blank.
Art and delusion are the same.
You look at me as if I am talking in code.

The hatchet inside roughs out a man.
In this tedious country I could think great thoughts,
Lily pads of words over the years.
Genius snaps in as narrative until everything is misplaced.

Do you ever feel more solid than in sadness?

VI
My teeth are my theme.

The body is to poetry as the eye is to breath.

Youth was polished troubles.

Good ideas are the clutter of bad discipline.

One idea cures a billion parts of despair.

Shop is the motherhood of metaphor.

Poems are reality mileage.

The miracle of our world is that we get our fortune *after* we eat.

Each year your grave is deeper by an inch.

The badge to write doesn't defend reality.

Would you rather stand by the door or the window?

VII
Each poem starts with a lament.

While remembering everything at once, the next
Ten thousand years begin in the life of poetry's death.

The maps have changed and everyone has new haircuts.
And we all imitate perfect form: wreathed
Words and bunting phrases, half-thought, half
Mastered until one sleeps a dolphin's sleep, the other one
Surfacing to breathe, giddy with the art of twice watching
The other dream, rutting urgency, and so on, to the end of water.
Now to sweep the brane, with wild
Impulse and reckless estimation.
I always feel like I'm writing
Last words. The risk is no words, wasting the time
Of future explorers. You,

The anthropologist of your own mind.

VIII
Thieves call for you.
Risk and breath.
My fragments and deliverance
meet and pass in an obsolete
language
as if unwritten.
Take all
the risk you can take.

IX

The moth sleeps in the spirals of my notebook.

Forty months without a poem. The stacks
Of unread books become gravestones, after all.
I'd almost forgotten the sensation of music. I shout
Through the wires, "I am, I am"—thousands
Of faces, responses, till the exhaustion
Of language. Language is a trampoline.
Heater pilot, like timpani, announces electric fan
As a symphonic opening. Think of the world
As a circuit for skittering sounds.
What bad habits were once kept in check, now sleep
Out of earshot.

The burden of syntax: it cannot be revised out of you.
Now is the turnaround. Fix-up a storm.
Wait in the dark for the next perspective.

X

It's as if your heart, expanding in heart alone,
Became the body's meal and feast.
The windows open onto the soft trough
And parked cars fail to shop and the migrations
To domestic accounts follow the dark wave.
In the bucket leak you see your poverty fill.
You see life as it is, reduced to its breaks.
This liquid rushes the house and soaks the timber.
Poetry in a recession: if you spend poverty,
You buy reality. It's so calm and cool.
The risk of being right is the same as
Predicting the time of night
Without a watch. If one could only sleep.

XI
It was Aphrodite's wish, the world turning
From me. But it was in the people
Where her unhappiness lived. How many
Quiet folk in coats know this? Bodies, loving,
Make the illusion "live." We've been asleep
In a boat. Beyond the green glacier walls, obscured
A week by fires, there are buffalo
Through the pass. If ankles were ears,
We'd hear the journeys they did not take.
The frame of time is too broken to use, so what's a moment for?
You don't survive the seasons here, you sing them.

A heavy winter with dry winds flew all day down
The chute of Highway 138. I'm armed
For opposites and, instead, am given contrasts:
Poppy orange and Lupine purple, yellow and violet
Surrounded by Teddy Bear Cactus. The heat and wind will
Take us back. Waking is a dream you might as well have.
On every corner you see green—it says, "Walk."
Yet, on any day, the poem is made in the walk,
Proving the poet never is, always just was.
My attention is larger than my cycle of days,
But a row of open caskets are your days.

Three Years of a Good Habit

From the Air

The not-caught trout was one reason for visiting
The lakes, traveling all this way. The Forest Service road
You saw from the air on an eastbound flight: your day
Changed. Hunters, Sheikhs, Spanish families dating to Cortez,
New Mexico, the continent's mother-skin on
Our surface. The road climbs to a widened height, a nifty
Imax shot: world river, the Rio Grande carving
The spilled Jemez volcano in a basin rushing to the Gulf
And a rainstorm with lightning snarling, a space
Free of contingency and association by its width.
The road leads to an excess of forest and, eventually,
Coyote, but I turn back to modern Santa Fe, swallowed
In the basin, rain gone. Home, the door open wide, air
Flowing through. I check for small animals.

Owens Valley

You're so principled you drive your family around
In your work truck on Sundays, trying to survive
Survival. Air covers snow which covers wise granite,
Which loses to space unless gravity's bending is
Always toward goodness. Elk yawn on cattle fields
And nobody chases them off. We're west of Lone Pine
In Creation's Crater where you can't climb higher
In the South 48 and I can't yet speak. Experience
Is wasted on the old. Rotten nostalgic. Flying
Down the highway at eighty, a high profile Lexus changes lanes
To avoid a classic Pontiac making a slow left turn in the fast
Lane. I hit the brakes as it flies toward me. There's
Room on the right to go around. My nephews are asleep,
So they miss the death I steer by. I trust my reactions,
Not my luck. The mountains must have laughed at my haste.
Assisted by his dog, a cowboy moves his cattle around
In the field. The mountains now sleep under stars, hoping
People get there some day and tell of mountains here.

The California Loop

The climbing mountain turns to a chemical lake.
No interest in description. This is blue
Among the gases . . . now I'm inclined to talk.

I've given up the wagons in the sand.
The horses have turned into grazers, not pullers.
They'll have to save themselves, perhaps a brigade
          of settlers.

All my strength is needed in crossing to Nevada.
No one has pioneered this direction, from Owens
Out toward Ely—I can't say why, either, but it puts us

Free of the California loop of the inside skin
And we arrive fully hinged and studded.
The house on the hill can slide or endure.

What we come back to is earth and fish.
I'll find some way to be happy. Perhaps go
Pull out the wagons, find someone interested
          in a ride.

Clever Desert

Years of our desert.
A leaning tree.
Swollen doors and topped-off
pools of rain. The street
is free of danger
of fire. The animals are outside.
The tortured prayer.
Mind-readied.
You think someone
would have prepared for
what to do in a stillness.
The water says
we don't need as much.
One fallen tree floats by.

Ghost Cradle

The house will wash away, the squalor in the yard,
the city and its pleasure slaveries into the sea.

The house had no new babies for years. One night
our five-year-old was over at a friend's. We heard

a crying baby on the baby monitor. I thought
a homeless family had camped downstairs. I woke

prepared to aid as any parent would, but the cry
was from an infant somewhere in the neighborhood

on the same frequency as ours. Give us, house, this
second chance to grow, this cry you filch from the night air.

After Rain

Dark cat's eyes look blue. The sky
Is an upside down lake with two stars.

Those inland seas came from sloshing, not uplift.
The fissure grows with rain, tilts the swing.

The weather seems like a prelude to judgment,
Good or bad. Faces on TV and tasks, part

Atmosphere, part book. The phone rang
In my dream to prolong time. People laugh in

Disbelief, know it's supposed to be night.
I spend my vacations not thinking about these

Things. The story always ends the same:
Lumber endures as forests, immobile,

Corresponding in all corners of the Earth,
Coloring maps. A hum passes through my speakers.

They are not turned on. News passes through us invisibly,
Even while we are thinking. The world of receding

Tides was happiest at 2AM. Just because the sun is
Shining, doesn't mean it's day, astronauts say. They

See waves better from high up. The dog barks at
Something I cannot hear. According to my temperament,

The sun should rise undetected, through stars.

You Are Always Entertaining and Delightful

"We no sooner get into the second Chamber, which I shall call the Chamber of Maiden-Thought, than we become intoxicated with the light and the atmosphere."

—John Keats

First Sun

I
I was wondering what I was doing a lifetime
Of 6:30 AMs when I finished this. Boat and wake
Sliding across the bay, day flickering with different
Weather when sunlight comes through the same room
And a figure picks up the same object to revolving, repetitive
Music. Dark, light, dark

Through the season. You're here for air.
This could be happiness, the moment
Just after, though it may be gone forever,
Or just before, like a grid of downtown
Windows bouncing first sun
That made you hear your father's voice
Saying get back on the straight path, you fool.

The early arrival of day, in darkness, borrowed
From year-days of silence at this hour, like phosphors
On a screen in the corners, never exposed
To television. It's a dance of the dead
For all the scribblings I couldn't decipher or add
To conversation with my dad when we got up
Half an hour early before fishing. What if we all got up
Half an hour early before the end of the world, and this is it?
Batteries in stacked tape recorders
Try to hold their charge while words
Flee to the future and can never be taken back, even
If unread. This isn't entropy, but its opposite.

Real Time

II
Here, the enemy
Of success is habit, not invalidation.
This story evolves in real time: the comedy
I left behind and abandoned was written to get girls,
Here or gone, the same, a face of entertainment.
Hear that breeze out there?
It could be our century's hurricane, or the still
Of peace where I raise my hand
From the page and wonder if my handwriting
Is legible. I write my message under my hand
So it reads like thought. My hand writes
With the rhythm of water.

Avoid meetings where there are more than two people.
Show your face in pictures, wave and gesture
That nothing is past. Underwrite
The reach for light like the blind. Now go
Forth and fill it with myth, music.
Welcome to the shadow and light that make no sound.
It helps perspective that we never move.
This is where we stop.
This is my story. This is my title.

The Future Is Not Destination

III
Grab me from this role.
What kind of sickness got me into this business?
I should start out all over.
I'm getting out with papers in both hands,
The sound of pencil and paper as reassuring as breath.
Run sun up and down for best clouds.
I'll put on "happy birthday" and cry
Myself awake. I'm going to wear my unfinished suit
To the agency today. This ordeal of starting left me
Breathless. The person you're not noticing
Carries the secret to the future. I'm this
Wincey smile in this picture. To say be quiet
Would have ruined it. I squeegee water beads
Off fishing line all day and think of it as my work.
I spend my time making casual jokes
And cartoon illustrations. I hold up a black VHS jacket.
"Is this 2001?" Someone
Would call this a job; I call it fore-forgetting, a way
To insure the future is not destination,
But rhythm, a warrior's dance
With only your message hacked in code
On limbs of bone. For fiction
And odd art no one dares set foot
In the factory.

The watchful present is only
Different by what it is unwilling to see:
The memory of memory.

Scene: An Ocean View

IV
The audience then shuts off at room temperature.

The subject of what you are working on comes up.
Everyone sees why you sought freedom
Through gravitation. It was a world
You could float away from, because it spells transition
Into iterative gloom where I've harpooned my theme.

Memory contains longing.
I'll hear the bird of January.

I'm in a field collecting doorstops, rising
White ocean, white, calm as palms.
Everywhere, people in light fit for photographs.

Body Caught by Light

V
I awoke in mid-air.
I wished for Mozart, to see spring on the screen,
To hear the sound of your own writing, the sound
Of traffic, slow moan. It is the theater
Of inconsequence: standing at the door, the lawn
Not moving, weighed by dew.

A day can be made from one thing falling.

Scene from Inside

VI
I had to climb over the top of the door
To get in. There was a dumb meeting going on
And I stopped it and a young Friend (F) I always liked.
She showered and let me soap her
As she talked of her lover, an older woman.
I can't remember how I got back into the house,
But everyone was eating and nothing
Is ever resolved and a man turns to me and says,
"In the commercial they hand you a cigarette
And tell you that you have 30 days to live. Here,
I hand you this table."
I turn and start kissing my wife.

The Text

VII
The process unfolds over days. Poor typing.
Only one handwritten copy handed around so fast
It blurred. The actors sat puzzling. At first,

There was no performance. The light popped with a flash
And there was vengeance, reason's charred *tienda*.
How long can you step off the plates

Until they move by you? Each day
You rise and eliminate the excess
Of yesterday's hope. Then, standing at the elephant

Door, the bright light hits your face . . . it's artificial, but
Everyone delights in the cliché. Special
Performances linking gestures, anchoring backstops; when

You're tired, you string out the A's, B's and C's
As mere behavior wins all beauty contests.
Work is a default holding out against lesser expression,

What's left trying to stand next to its cousin, perfection.
The actors wander through carefully, stepping between
Magazines that stick to their feet, crying for opportunity.

I'll spend the day gathering more unseen records,
Placing them in possible order. Indecipherable? Welcome
To the *arrety-hell* (sp) of abstract self-expression.

The only flaw in good work is
Broken concentration.

Scene: San Francisco, Day

VIII
Boats in bay. Puffy clouds.
Everything is subtext as in "we got you here to see
Clowns but actually it's about priests."
The light on shoulder, that hair cut around the ear:
Who is that man and what does he want? I see
The nose bridge and eyes thinking, footsteps racing
To something nearly missed. Where is he?
He looks around as if in a great epic.
He is lost and it is funny. Then
The ordinary hides the meaning and no matter
What happens, funny or unfortunate, it's the vignettes.
This guy is standing here and no one will notice
In one hundred years. There's a scene, standing
There, knowing that. We think he is just standing there
Though some think he's sexy and that's what it's about.
Fine execution by nature at least, widescreen,
Clean lines, white building, clouds,
Alcatraz. He calls in, wrong Starbucks, wrong
Side of town, oh my, but the other party canceled.
It's now comedy. He stands and looks at the bay.

Asleep on the Pacific

IX
I'm atmosphere in local dress, in and out
Of pictures. The first rain
Brings panic. Did we invent
Bad driving? I lift self
Unspent and unsaved
Into a new day. Perhaps the mind
Has migrated in it's own medium
To sit at the surface, seeking air or pleasure.
Then the movie shows the scene where sailors
See land and the black hole of crashing surf.
But that's just content.
My purpose isn't plot or place, but idiom's cousin,
Fabric.

I live by the widest river in the world,
The Pacific, so wide the continents float by.
At night, blinking at stars, I set for the swim to shore.
How early to be old, how old to be young.
The goddess and her companion were lost
All day having chosen the wrong canyon,
Cried from exhaustion at the blank sea's mind.
It's not an empty room . . . but
A circle where I float away with my things
And the gentle illusion we tried to make of the island.

Tobogganing the Opera House

X
A gardener braves the swaths of ten thousand silent
Leaves of grass. (Whitman in charge of greens.)

Today: put the woodpile on stilts, dislodge
The rodent and bumblebee nest within the wood.
The bees flew as I stoked bare-handed, but didn't sting.

Setup.

We looked for a place to sled.
The Opera House parking lot was the best choice.
The gate was locked, no gaps to skinny through.
All other terrain too steep and rapid ending
In arroyo. We found a path through juniper
And piñon, a creeping path, not swift and jolly.
Called it a day, lying there in Gore-Tex on top of snow.

Next setup.

I turn and walk with charm (it's a backdrop),
Lugging orchids to school and back. You leap to Germany
Street. There's a cow in the basement.
It's around Easter and the fog is stacked to heaven,
And deep gray. We travel the countryside and see
No poverty. Birds. Jackhammer on, jackhammer off.
A man walks through the group heading for the ocean,
carrying a pole and a bucket. The sky opens wide.

We could have slept till summer as if
Grain grew and rolled about fields of headstones.
The sea is falling, not the sky.

When the water rushes out of the bay, we notice
Everyone has been swimming naked.

Boat I Liked: My Movie

—Beauty is the best leverage.

XI
Boat I liked docked
next to ours at departure.
Dingy left us on shore, party by party, decimated
by the heat, hat burn, ears buzzing with cicadas
of the blood, no landmarks
except people passing — the frail animal-commerce
clouds the awe and we don't really know
what century this is.

There's one boat home
each year and I just missed it. I screen all day.
I can't have my freedom and my art
so I've lost track of the feeling for what time
of day it is. There's not an hour you don't regret
pushing further, a camera looking back at you
and these objects, monitors, cups, books and papers, are the lens
that includes you, a moment invisible to all who watch,
audible to yourself and your dog
as something strange and familiar.

I'm eliminating the side effects, listing
the credits; the bloggers have it worked out beforehand, and
I haven't fallen in love with my main character yet.
Let me now embarrass you with my emotion.
I inherited the vanity sport by watching.
We trick vanity from others.
Photos point at a small history.
Another season closes. This

fabulous hive of happiness of enterprise is
about to break. Scatter the ships in the Pacific.
We'll be affluent slaves. You're compared to
the boulder man of Arizona. Your charisma, seen
or unseen, is to place rock on rock in space.
Let's talk about sex now.

Vanity Sport

XII
I inherited the vanity sport by watching
The green hills of Burbank become the amber of tourist
Parks, dream backlots high-rise and apartment slum.
Here we are looking dormant, all of our art out-of-style
As the new cities burst in the hemisphere with
Nobody, I mean nobody, claiming the center.
Again, I start out with lead point to page

Ten thousand snapshots of wrists behind me.

Polishing an image, I encounter
Glass — but this had never, in a lifetime, let
A surface show, except a darkened screen.

Painting was achieved by placing equally
Empty volumes behind the screen to assert,
In real time, a record of the empty flow.

It's magic hour in Universal City.
The cars stuck in traffic bounce golden light,
And fill the senses with the memory of movies.
I slide home, turning the radio from lack of sleep,
Adjusting the visor.

Laurel Canyon, Houdini's Mansion

XIII
Vines grow on the outside walls.
You pause and tip into the dilemma, stripped
Of all gear and defenses, a rope on your feet, upside
Down into the tank, then plywood nailed
All around. You and the purged circle come
To see this march when wearing
Your musical ear.

Time passes like a swallow.

No new coin or last minute saves.
Come, edit me and chop the little
Pieces into a picture like a bar of winter light
Into a dark room where people would rather sleep.

You have mastered the hour
Against a decade of sure forgetting.
To walk to the wall then touch it, walk through.
You know the inside and what you touch,
Can't see or name it, then there
You stand, in front of us.

Picture within Picture

XIV

The test for an ending is to see if it's original.

You realized down the way to an elevator
Cage, watching as you weave
Together happenstance and randomness,
You are a moment. As anyone can see
The background story sustains our interest.
I think I found a limit to perception:
I could not listen to the lunch specials
While trying to recognize a stranger's face

As he turned around, some distance from my table,
Can't listen to two musics simultaneously either.
If we counted *down* our years we would surely live
More cautiously. So write a day, think forever.
I see myself falling asleep.
I need a morality when pleasure is all that's left
And dwindling time. The machine sweeps me in
As I drive dying cars. Organizers know the perfect
Weather for skywriting. Pictures of our age
Will be conspicuous due to the absence of robots.
This month's been like no other culture.

When the Industrial Revolution Ended

The Street Is a Pile of Entropy

The street is a pile of entropy with everything
You and your nineteenth century partners amassed.
I don't want to get up and tell you about the bad
Situation, but can't distract my mind from images
Of catastrophe and the coming of an American century
Rising from the twisted wreckage of the WTC.
On a farm in Nebraska where crows fly over snowy
Corn, the winter has come, and there, out of the soil,
The intense and fibrous light of the virtuous
Underground streams to the surface. The land
Is indifferent to plant and artifact, and human
Life recedes behind this bunker of light.
Nobody flinches at the sight of airplanes now.
This is not Science Fiction, this is what remains of us after
We pause for Disney, Proctor, Gamble, the Gap.
Our protection is our simple life indoors, cleansing
The well, fixing the grain to the calendar, making
The world talk in unison, simple speed of civilization.

M. I.

A beautiful silence. I'm lighter
than I've been in
New York City. I'm awake,
and this is an average
place where you stop to help the lost.
It's so silent my ears ring like
sirens. Hallway, corridor, elevator, street,
Gramercy cab patterns disrupted by a walk.
Rucksack and cell and pleasure plastic,
I watch every person. We're not a beautiful
cosmos. On Great Jones, a sink rests
in the street. On every block
an armature of coffee. Come here, it says.
From space it's the ring finger.

When the Industrial Revolution Ended

I haven't seen gray suits since the '70s.
The pill upholstery compares to a tube
Bent round, entering itself and forgetting
A dimension: the boundary up, beside and down.
That's why, when we pull apart our troubles,
We forget, and start again. We are crawlers
Inside and think of it as heaven when the direction
That is most free is made of our own hardware.
If I can't look up it's because the city gets to me.
I'll smile my commercial smile, but that building
Over there just squatted on folks. Once I was a hawk
Amid tall buildings where place is just a climate
With the same neighbors: the boundary up, beside
And down is ignored again. The generals are shooting
In all directions, armies of water drops rush the house,
The machines synchronize flawlessly, the face
Is clean. Yes, we are all about preparations.
They don't know what happens in tubes. A generation
Cries as it pulls up the limp rope of its former hope.

Independence Day

The cars slip back like pebbles into the well
And this summer light makes it easy to please the chilly
At parties here, inside the gallery corridor without art.
I hope I'm right that the event should be on
Her turn, not mine—then, suddenly, I hear
Someone shout "freeze," and if that didn't get
Our attention, the off-course blimp advertising
Movies swept into power lines at just that moment.
Things change, as it did for the ditching students
Who saved lives, became class heroes, made papers.
The calls linked bad parents who dressed their kids
Too cute with trick toys, whose wealth was paradox.
Eras with allergies, urban exploration. I'm freezing from
Unknown temperature in the brick of the Brooklyn Bridge.
Give me serum of the censorious beast out
In the flats that watches our TV, but can't shop
Our cracked and shouting strip malls.

Transparent Junkyard

Built by ex-Romans where time runs backwards
Until all is stone. It's Chicago. It's the present.
I change my mind like a tourist, waking in the dark
Before knowing the weather, forgotten like a zoo
Upon leaving. I resign to everything in a circle until
Giving is going out. Have you seen the countryside
Flowers hidden in storms? It was a quick winter
There and the view is spectacular from here.
But don't freeze me; it's cruel and I'm not moving,
Ear to the wall. By now the birds are up and the Western
Tanager is today's feathered migrant. It's small with red head,
Black wing and arresting yellow breast. Money is a bird
In a tree. The part of life that can be perfected, isn't.
We are born and die twenty-five miles from home. The dead should
Wear a sign, "You are Free." Between clean and cluttered
There's no middle road.

The Term "Homo Sapiens"
Is Reserved for Those Over 50

With all these new people running
Around, you'd think they'd all be born
Remembering something. It's a joke
If you knew what happens. The body
Fits the lock of the door you open.
All you do is die, mid-sentence, wait
Without pleasure, herding the young,
perfecting works. Ask me questions.
Three-thousand engineers are solving
Impossible problems beyond our use and
Ping, goes the excellent life. Another
Wide sunrise with red jets. We're elevated
Again and again. It's the fault of winglessness
That this air is not our only habitat.

Specially Woven Edge That Prevents
Cloth from Unraveling

In the wind machine, at the ranch, the bristle
cone canyon that blows day after day—I'm halfway
away from where I started
   an hour ago.
I'm merry and cannot work. I'm surrounded
by comic hybrids, cologned, listening to music! Precise
speech makes me feel
   still in school. Yonder lathering
doctors make surgery less medieval. The future
is here, living between the genius and the challenged.
I cause myself to love mankind.
   I'm one of us.
I rush around, too, civilization, a real estate thing
for owners. I'm still aware of my extremities, of everything
like habit. Time having never left
   passes faster when not passing
   old growth further by branches from new seed.
   I'm aware and unprepared in the selvages.
If there could be some conclusion, it would buy my
one holiday year of salutary
   forgetting and cutting.

Hunting for Orchestras

I

By now yellows have found their blues, blacks
Their whites, nothing its randomness.

She arches her back to emphasize her green
Breasts, her ennui. They are decorated in

Beaded circles to her neckline. I woke
To a new sky. This is the missing week.

The coffee is too thin for a quorum. I placebo
Myself by holding my nose. The ringing phone

Is part of a dream. Being in a world is not enough.
Profits are time. Become time as you live.

I've bottled all the flies I can find.
I was given 4,000 days to be a lad.

I command that my powers be at their peak
By my fiftieth year. It is my fiftieth year.

Now that the fan is off I hear my own blood and
I'm happier with new meaning than old language.

I sit and write in the same cruel circle of days
Against the thought that the words will reveal my cause—

I've always meant my morning to reciprocate
For the generous fantasies of sleep. Thank you.

II

The manqué of romance passes like a virus.
Anger before sun-up. The unusual, please . . .

It's a suit without pockets and a liquid that makes you forget
Fractures. Your squeaky smile betrays your gloom.

It's nice to be back on the bold perspective roadway.
It's as if there were myself in every object, exhorting.

Faster, higher, stronger! My hurricane breath
(to small spiders) creases as I sigh and howl

Below thunder noggin. The heat and drought
Impoverish like a diet of rats. Now, name

A place that doesn't evoke food. Yesterday's
Happiness, behind a bunker of light, was the absence

Of conflict, not the pizza of forgotten cheese, meditation
With a prize. Say grace before you speak in asperities.

III
You arose not knowing today was the day
You would record. The opinions come out

Like fake trash to be picked up after it is over.
Dog bowl, banjo. There are so many intelligent,

Yet so few exemplary people. I'm not quiet today,
Though I haven't said a word. Axioms, shy

From over-application, reject the wheels–on–cows premise.
The need of the day is to not walk smirking into complexity.

I don't know about you, but I'm seeing ridiculous
But lovable characters saying these things.

I turn out the lights so I do no illustrate myself.
I'll probably just stop suddenly to see if someone's listening . . .

Birds probably sit there and crack stupid jokes all day.
I always feel I owe them something. A tip? Lawsuits race

Through the mind that would injure worse by binding you
To injury. Who resigns to complaints at last achieves a career.

Success doesn't need a vacation. I raided my life to live it.
Haven't got used to stars. My happiness makes them hungry.

How far is that mountain? Again I rise fleeing from myself
And some cussing argument about duty to a tree.

I realize after all these years sleep has been a waste.
In dreams you do not see edges. Are you happy?

IV
These carefree days are not relief from work.
It's an insane paradise, our stiff city, with no public places

To sprawl. Leave it all behind like steaming ships.
The sleep that had the fraudulence of luck hides the pain

Of misfortune. Conduct would have fear rule, not hope.
Each step I take measures the distance of time gone.

A dog barks and hopes that another day will bring an opinion.
A tone born longs for another. Photographs reek with order.

In the still wrinkle of our place, it's the dream
Of days when poplars morphed from candles.

Standard

Time is no issue. There isn't a line at my door,
I'm well passed what–am–I–doing–here because
I don't have to be anywhere right now. It's Tuesday.

The gate stands open as if something's terribly wrong.
It isn't. Groceries. I rise forgetting. Was that rain?
I dread the continuity of each certainty, the way

Workers look at the clock. Nothing shook the hill
I live on, no houses float in the ocean. As I walk
To my village, I see commuters' lives blurred by cars

And trains. I left this behind in a hurry. Disoriented
By the annoying change in time, I arrived early,
Deserted. Quiet. Gardener rustling. Garbage truck.

A Yard Full of Holes

Start the ritual dance. Just sheets by now raining fields
Deep with spring. Here come the Monarchs, here
Come the gulls. It's Mr. Eastside braking for the beach,
Already hot. You missed it in the idle/pleasant dry spell,
Sprinklers needed for crust. And a new man, yellow this time,
Inventing power from tides, husking beach frost from a comic
Seal, glad that land seals are dogs, too. There was the long year's
Reward before you, a bird clicking a timer that you cannot bury
In a drawer. Shut it off, all off, till you hear the gate open down
At the Mexican border. I've rescued the day without bracing
The myth. You are the smiling riddle you can't crack
And the months prove nothing with proverbs. Sometimes
It's enough to come home with the news of water.

Search Lights in the Valley

There's always a chance the sparest strategy
Of saying what crosses the mind will leave behind
A rock in words. Airplanes and blimps, jumbo jets traverse
This sky while cars and buses move below. My searchlight
By day glints the flying chrome, the radio tower, the over-
Sized billboard saying, *Hurry!* Which I aid not. But
Everything changed in a minute. I could not have
Anticipated rain this summer, the rain of February.
Helicopters patrol the beach, women postpone their make-up
For traffic, a clip of sun on glass, the end. I'm released and walking
On a dirt road in the shade of a long June night. I find something
On the road, not a rock, not metal, the meteorite of years.

My Summer Started

. . . and everything amazed, no villa, no dairy, no one
Named Dale or in one, it happened over Memorial Day
And our Papa let go of his grief, no other explanation.
He went back to times when it was fun, grapes and dogs
And an oar out of every window in the village, everyone
Just moving along. I remember watching his best
Dog wake up one early morning, that moment when
She had to confront herself and thirst, apart from dream.
I felt bad because she would die before us,
So the facts were correct for her. Her white tail wagged
At first sight of other people. It's back to normal
With the old idiom, with new tourists who yearn to be
Touched, and at a time when you can take yourself
Seriously again. It's agriculture after all, taste not test,
Next door a dairy, not a diary.

It was Sweden for blonde times.

Notes:

★ http://www.space.com/scienceastronomy/astronomybigbang_alternative_010413-1.html